Lilli Höch-Corona

King Archibald
and the Gefühlsmonsters

Little colorful creatures
that no one has ever seen

Copyright: © 2023 Lilli Höch-Corona

Gefühlsmonster GmbH

Bornholmer Straße 19

10439 Berlin

Editing: Erik Kinting – www.buchlektorat.net

Illustrations: Christian Corona

Cover & typesetting: Sabine Abels

Publisher and printer on behalf of the author

tredition GmbH, Heinz-Beusen-Stieg 5, 22926 Ahrensburg, Germany

Softcover 978-3-384-01043-8

Hardcover 978-3-384-01044-5

E-Book 978-3-384-01045-2

 # Preface

Does this sound familiar? A friend complains to you about a terrible other person – and somehow, as you listen, the impression arises in you that the friend also has a share in this problem ...

The first version of this fairy tale was written eight years ago. I had observed the theme of not being aware of one's effect on others again and again in others or in myself and I wanted to encourage people in a metaphorical way to rethink.

Here are a few episodes from my work that show where this topic has crossed my path in my career: In my work at school, I noticed that there were students who "bothered" some teachers and not others, regardless of whether the subject was interesting to them or not. Later, as a trainer for team development and conflict management, I was asked by teachers to get their students to interact better with each other. I almost always found that the way the teachers approached them played an important role. As a mediator, I experienced parents who felt misunderstood by their children and could not see their own part in it. Or that managers who asked me to mediate between their employees, were surprised when I asked to speak to the managers themselves.

Preface

In my preliminary conversations on team development in companies I started to ask the managers at the beginning whether they would be willing to participate in coaching as well. This was often refused. If it then became clear that there was a lack of clarity in the communication of the manager or in the team roles, or that there was an unconscious aversion to individual employees, my hands were bound without permission to also work with the manager.

At some point, I began to negotiate the consulting of the manager together with planning the team development, which led to much more sustainable results of this work. The prerequisite, of course, was an attitude of non-judgment, respect for the leaders and the reasons for their behavior. Then, when a side-by-side approach emerged, together we were always able to find solutions for all involved. Sometimes that included a manager changing careers or employees leaving the team in mutual agreement.

Over time, I found it more and more unfortunate when people reached a dead end because of their bias toward counseling. Students observe teachers very closely and have a very fine sense of fairness, likes and dislikes. It is the same with staff members, who sometimes know us better than we know ourselves. How can we embrace these valuable impulses?

Preface

All of us are sometimes unaware of how we affect others. Anyone who has children can tell you a thing or two about what precious and sometimes challenging "teachers" our children are to us ...

As a mediator, language is an important vehicle for me. My work is often a translation of the client's words spoken in anger. There is a good reason that finding the words that express an issue, including the feelings triggered, without judging either party to the dispute, makes up the main part of a mediator's education. This always requires an attitude of benevolence, in order to make a kind offering with these formulations, so that someone can understand something that they did not understand before. And: an offer can always be accepted or rejected.

Personal changes are only possible on a voluntary basis, in an atmosphere of respect, and if the persons can see and feel that the change is an improvement for them in the direction of their own values and wishes. This requires a lot of sensitivity and the understanding that there may be other ways than the ones I see as a counselor, or that the timing might not be the right one for the person being counseled.

Preface

I have always enjoyed reading beautiful stories that made me think and gave me images I could relate to. For example, Clarissa Pinkola Estes'[1] image of the seal woman who falls in love with a human and has to shed her skin to do so. I think that's a beautiful image of how we adapt in relationships. And how we then sometimes must find new ways to live "our sealskin".

Ed Watzke[2] has encouraged us to tell stories in mediations to draw people out of their well-worn paths. There is the story of the lighthouse that is radioed by a ship in the fog, asking it to get out of the way – completed with impressive ranks of the inquiring captain. This story has made me and some of my mediation clients smile about such persistence while being on the wrong track, and has caused many a rethink.

Another example is Jorge Bucay[3], whose therapy for a young man consisted entirely of storytelling and dialog about it.
Hanna Milling's "Storytelling[4]" is a treasure trove of stories for conflict resolution and counseling, carefully categorized by theme and impact, that has often been very helpful in my work.

....

1 Calrissa Pinkola Estes "Women who run with Wolves" page 256ff
2 Ed Watzke: "Wahrscheinlich hat diese Geschichte gar nichts mit Ihnen zu tun"
3 Jorge Bucay: "Let Me Tell You a Story: Tales Along the Road to Happiness"
4 Hanna Milling: "Storytelling – Konflikte lösen mit Herz und Verstand"

Preface

Through these experiences I grew a desire to write a fairy tale myself. My intent was to metaphorically draw attention to the dilemma between self-perception and the perception of others, and to recount the benefits of dealing with one's own feelings with humor. Even or especially if this feels very difficult or just impossible at the beginning. Getting to know one's own feelings – and all of them! – is the basis for self-acceptance, for love and for getting along with others.

Ideally, children are welcomed at birth and meet adults who love and guide them to thrive with their own desires and potentials, so that they know what they need for their well-being and how they can contribute to their community.

This process is very easily disrupted, and not only children born during or soon after war times do not have this safety net within themselves. (To expand on this is beyond the scope of this book.) Emotions then sometimes appear unexpectedly as an "attack" and are so difficult to handle that we often choose not to feel them[5]. Our environment, however, perceives them, and this can result in conflicts that are challenging to deal with.

---

5   More about this in my book "Sometimes Feelings are Monsters"

Preface

I was drawn to making a not so helpful behavior lovingly understandable, so that it is acceptable through metaphorical contemplation. That is what I wish for my story!

In my work I have encountered more men than women who showed traits like King Archibald. Therefore, the hero of this story is a king.

I hope that the twinkle in my eyes and the loving look at the behaviors we sometimes exhibit in the course of our personal development shine through.

Whether we show these behaviors as leaders to whom the king alludes, as parents, or simply as the person we are and strive to master life.

Of course, it could just as well be a queen visiting another queen, and her husband would be the one to help her get to know better these *little, brightly colored creatures that no one has ever seen …*

Once upon a time there was a King ...

Once upon a time there was a king named Archibald, who had a lot of stupid loyal subjects. Unbelievable, how much mischief they created! When the king was in a generous mood, they took it the wrong way and were suspicious. When the king was angry, they didn't even see what they had done wrong and instead gathered in secret behind his back, weaving tales of ill will.

Many times had Archibald summoned a grand assembly of the people, intending to guide his subjects on how to live happily and content in his realm. He meant nothing but kindness towards them! Yet, what did they do? It seemed they had beans in their ears, misunderstanding everything he said and refusing to see the wisdom in his words.

And then his third queen had left him – understand these bewitching women, if you can! Although he was such a benevolent king, and nothing pleased him more than doting on his beautiful queen, she had accused him of lacking empathy for her royal emotions, and that was much too bad.

The king was so desparate that he decided to embark on a journey of wander and wonder, seeking advice beyond his kingdom's borders. He had heard of a distant kingdom where the royal subjects were

very clever, and he wanted to go there to learn from this king how his own subjects could become smart like that. So that he could age gracefully, surrounded by love from all, just as he had always wished in his heart.

After a long, exhausting journey on his horse he arrived at King Frederics kingdom, was warmly welcomed, fed, and slept soundly in an amazingly soft bed. What had this king done that his servants did such good work? They were friendly and courteous; indeed, it seemed that they enjoyed their work! King Archibald was excited to learn what strategies King Frederic had used to achieve this.

The next morning, he was allowed to attend the king's daily audience as a guest. Unbelievable how polite these people were! As soon as they saw their king, they laughed

11

happily, reported on their successful achievements, asked him questions that he was happy to answer, and answered his questions. Indeed, they even presented their children, which, as everyone knows, has no place in a royal audience!

Nobody looked around cautiously before they stepped in front of the king, nobody had lowered their eyes or wrung their hands anxiously. It was unbelievable. What a lucky guy! And, to top it all off, he had a beautiful queen by his side, graced with enchanting charm!

This king was so fortunate! If only he could be so lucky, thought Archibald.

While he waited for Frederic to attend to other government business, Archibald went for a walk in the castle's park. He laid down behind a beautiful, large rose bush and fell asleep.

When he awoke, he saw little brightly colored creatures under the rose bush that he had never seen before. As he perked up in amazement, he noticed that they were talking to each other very, very softly.

"Hee-hee," said one of them, "have you heard that a new king has arrived and wants to learn from Frederic? If he just knew! It took so long for Frederic to become a smart king! Will the new king be able to learn? Who knows?"

"Do you remember," they told each other laughing, "how King Frederic used to look at his audience and wondered why his subjects had no confidence in him?"

"Or how he used to tell the queen, when she confided her worries to him, to not take it to heart? Oh, it took quite some time for him to grasp that the queen felt differently than he did, and that his strength didn't ease her burdens either."

"And how annoyed the king was with the master of the manor who misunderstood everything he was supposed to do?"

"It was so difficult to show the king that he scared the master of the manor with his approach, making him so anxious that he could not remember what the king had said!"

"In this case we explained to the king in some of our evening consultations that a person needs to feel calm to be able to remember things or to have clever ideas."

They seem to be quite cheeky!, thought King Archibald. *How disrespectful they talk about this wonderful king! As if they knew everything better!* Which, as everyone knows, cannot be, because, after all, the king is the brightest in his kingdom. *I'll tell Frederic about it right away,* he said to himself, *because he doesn't seem to know what's going on in his realm. Outrageous little colorful beings! In a kingdom!*

When our king told Frederic about his experience during dinner he was astonished when Frederic remarked laughingly about Archibald having met his little advisors already.

"You may go and study with them with my permission," said Frederic.

"But take heed, for they are elusive creatures. If something displeases them, they vanish for a long time and are seen no more!"

The next day King Archibald went into the garden again. He sat down quietly on the bench next to the rose bush and waited. And, you guessed it, one of the creatures came up to him, a quite friendly one. It stood in front of him and said: "Our esteemed King Frederic has told us that you have come to learn from us how to govern your kingdom with joy and how to get along well with people. Is that what you want to learn? Can you imagine that during the next while you will listen to us and patiently wait until we have explained everything to you?"

"Yes, yes," Archibald said, trying hard not to show his impatience, because he had hoped that King Frederic would explain his government rules to him so he could soon ride back home to his own kingdom. *Hm. He was supposed to learn from these little colorful creatures? Tiny creatures that no one had ever seen? Quite strange. Maybe Frederic was playing tricks on him?*

Before he knew it, the little creature had disappeared, and no matter how much he searched around the castle garden, on this day Archibald never saw one again.

In the evening, at dinner time, he asked Frederic to understand that he, as an established king, really could not listen to such tiny, brightly colored creatures and waste his time with them. He pleaded him to just tell him how he ruled so he would be able to emulate everything finely.

It was too bad that Frederic smiled when he heard this:
"Dear Archibald, unfortunately I can't help you there! Without the little creatures, I will not succeed in making you understand the most important rules of dealing with the people in your kingdom. It took quite a long time for me to listen to them, because I,

too, was an impatient king. Imagine, I always thought it was wasted time when they came and wanted to show me something. Then they disappeared again until I was so desperate that I went looking for them again." Archibald's eyes widened in astonishment.

"If you like I can tell you how I learned to listen to them," Frederic continued. "It was many years ago, when a terrible disease broke out in my kingdom. How annoying it was, when my servants fell ill, the farmers ceased their toil, and we were deprived of milk and fresh meat. At first I tried to use threats to get someone to continue meeting our royal needs, and when all else failed, I brought up my chests of gold from the cellar and tried to get people to work for me by showering them with gifts. But much sooner than I had thought, the royal chests were

empty and no servant was to be seen far and wide, because
they were all ill or with their sick families. When my dear
queen fell ill and often angrily sent me out of her room when
I wanted to encourage her, I was in despair. I sat down in the
very back of the garden, in an overgrown corner behind an
old rose bush and wept in deep grief. I, the king!"

King Archibald frowned a little. *Why did Frederic tell him
all this?* But because he desperately wanted to know how
Frederic had managed to have such clever subjects, he
continued to listen.

 "And because I was so tired and desperate, I just sat there,
even though I was getting a bit frightened, because out of
nowhere these little brightly colored creatures appeared,
you already know them. I watched them dance and noticed
how I became calmer just by watching. It was as if I could
understand deep inside my body what they were showing
me with their dance and songs, as if not my ears but my
whole body was listening. And that felt a bit scary on one
hand, but really beautiful on the other."
 Archibald pondered for a moment, for he hadn't
paid attention to that at all, being immediately
annoyed by the disrespectful words of the tiny
people.

"They were singing about joy and happiness and how nice it is to be connected with one another. That then everyone helps each other because they want to do that. And that you could learn this by listening with your heart."

Archibald felt quite uncomfortable. What was this all about? This was not at all what he had expected. This amazing King Frederic was telling him very strange things ...

"And what can I tell you? Suddenly I felt these little creatures inside of me! One felt quite warm,

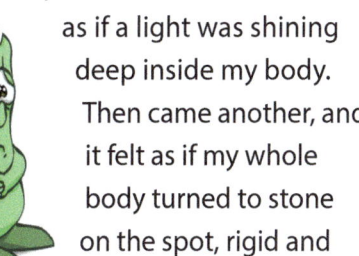

as if a light was shining deep inside my body. Then came another, and it felt as if my whole body turned to stone on the spot, rigid and

immovable. That hurt quite a bit and filled me with fear. I ran away because I couldn't stand it."

That did not sound at all like a king who was successfully governing his kingdom. Archibald felt great inner turmoil that he could not explain. But, nevertheless, he continued to listen closely to Frederics narrative.

"The next time I dared to go back in the garden, there came another one that was painful! I quickly ran away and went to my wife to ask her to comfort me. It's hard to believe, but she said that these little mischief-makers, who instill fear and dread, hold the key to love and connection, and that putting up with them isn't so bad. She said that this painful feeling, if we dare to look and feel it in the body, only lasts for a little while and then it leaves again. She taught me that the moment I see this being, I should take three deep breaths, focus inside my body, take my time, and silently say to myself: *This is how it feels when I am afraid!* I took that to heart and so I was able to stay a little longer the next time. Each time I could stay a little bit longer. Over time I even named the creatures and welcomed the ones that caused me pain as well."

Slowly, the realization dawned upon
Archibald that he had been quite mistaken
in his belief that the subjects needed to
learn to be smart. Frederic was telling
a story about himself, the king!
Learning, enduring pain, feelings?!
Oh dear, oh dear ...

Frederic continued with the story.
Archibald could not help but listen
to it all.
"And guess what I do now when I feel
this creature that hurt me so much
back then? Because unfortunately,
this does happen every now and
then, for example, when I see
that I've done something wrong
or hurt another person. This
is part of being human and it
happens to all of us again and
again! And that is so painful! I
would rather not have known
that! But by now I've learned
to quietly tell myself: *Oh, there*

21

you are again, welcome pain! Because that's just how it feels when I hurt someone and that hurts me! I understood that sometimes I do make mistakes – and that this is normal! And if I can accept that the uncomfortable feeling leaves soon."

Making mistakes? The king? Archibald thought, being completely bewildered.

Frederic pretended not to notice this and continued, "Sometimes this creature also comes along when I scold and rant in my fury and ire: *Goodness and goblins, I've had enough! I must keep learning and learning, endlessly, and I'm still not done!*"

"*Yes, to grumble, that sounds just right.*" Archibald thought, "*I quite enjoy doing that.*"

"That still happens to me sometimes," Frederic continued. "What do I do then, you'll want to know? Well, I say to myself, *'Aha, that's what it feels like when I'm angry!'* And because I

then know that now my old self is whining because it would rather stay the way it was in the past, I am kind to it and say *YES, dear, it's alright, you're doing much better than before!* And every time I manage to

feel it inside of my body, this being leaves faster.
That makes it easier for me to welcome it when it
shows up again."

*Welcoming them? Never! These strange beings
that no one has ever seen ... Who would still
take me seriously?* Archibald thought to
himself. *But Frederic is such a successful
and happy king ... Something doesn't fit at
all!* And because he wished to unravel
this nonsense, he continued
to listen intently.

"I now know that if I'm not able
to endure this pain, I won't
notice when I'm really happy
either. Then I also don't notice
how someone else feels. And
then nobody likes me ... Over
time it got less difficult. You
can believe me, Archibald!
Especially, because again and
again these little beings sang
for me the most beautiful songs

that touched me deeply. Over time the rigid feeling that was so scary before slowly dissolved.

And how I marveled when suddenly, just like that, I found the little beings inside of me again in my day-to-day governing! When my dear queen got well again, I noticed how a warm, bright feeling, that I had never experienced before, was spreading throughout my body. This was awesome! So, in conversation with other people, I started to pay attention to feeling pleasant or rather unpleasant beings inside of me. And, imagine: sometimes I could even feel other people's feelings!"

Well, I certainly don't want that, Archibald thought to himself. *A king should only possess royal emotions!*
But Frederics next words captivated Archibald: now he was finally, finally talking about the subjects!
"When the first royal employees recovered and returned to work, it quite scared me to suddenly feel that they and other subjects feared me. That was terrible! And not at all right, whereas I had always been such a kindly king!"

Well, then I would be an unkind king. But that's not true at all! Archibald grumbled to himself.

"That's how hard it was for me! I was surprised then, when my dear queen helped me so much with how to tolerate these beings, and she shared with me how their appearance came about. Now I had the best help in understanding and learning to deal with the little advisors inside of myself and in others. Over time, all by itself, the royal employees became friendlier. To my surprise, they now worked much harder and soon the kingdom was doing better again. I couldn't have imagined that in my wildest dreams."

Aha, now he finally gets to the point. Better royal employees,
that's exactly what I want! But all this fuss ... And the way
Frederic talks, it's truly too much to bear ...

"I'm thrilled to have met these colorful
creatures," Frederic continued.
"I can't imagine what would have
happened otherwise! I now notice when
one of these creatures shows up and
that feels awesome to me. Yes, I'm even
proud of learning to become a better version
of myself. And that feels sooo good! Well, my
dear King Archibald, what do you think? Do
you want to study with them? Do you trust
yourself to be strong enough to get to know
even the scarier beings? For that is necessary
for you to get to know more and more of these
wonderful, loving creatures."

There's no way I'm going to do that!, Archibald thought
to himself. *There must be another way!* He
looked away feeling uneasy. Frederic understood
Archibald's concerns from his own experience and
said, "Think it over! You may accompany me for a
few months on my royal duties and join my evening

council meetings. As a matter of fact, I take their advice every evening! That way I can take the time to reflect on my day-to-day government business and on what's important for the next day, and I get a good night's sleep afterwards. If you stay close to me during the day, I can always let you know which creature is being felt inside of me at the moment. That way you can find the courage to believe me that it is not as unpleasant as it sounds at first."

After this long and strange tale King Archibald's inner frustration grew. *That was supposed to help? Who knew if his subjects would react exactly as Frederics did? Oh dear, oh dear …*

That night Archibald went to bed reflecting on all of these bizarre stories. And although his stomach hurt, he went to King Frederics royal audience the

next day and watched very closely. And it actually unfolded exactly the way he had always dreamed of!

The following year King Archibald went to visit King Frederic for a few days every so often, taking part in the evening council meetings and spending time in the palace garden with the brightly colored creatures.

Frederic had to encourage him every now and then to pay attention to the little creatures in his own kingdom as well, which Archibald found difficult at first. But it helped a lot to experience Frederic in his dealings with his subjects and with his queen.

Above all, over time Archibald learned to be more compassionate with himself. Being a good, smart king he had expected of himself to immediately implement everything he had learned – and somehow that just didn't work!

Frederic was very supportive, always praising him for his progress and encouraging him. Thankfully, he only spoke such things during their evening strolls in the kingdom's garden, where no one could hear, or it would have been truly too much to bear.

Archibald was very surprised when one day, during the evening round table with the advisors, some of the little colorful creatures stepped in front of him and said that they would now accompany him to his own realm, to aid him in establishing the same warm bond with his servants and his wife, just like King Frederic. What joy it brought!

There they all were, the ones he had come to know well over time: the pleasant and the painful – exactly the ones who could lend him their support! The next day he went home with them to his kingdom and looked forward to the evening consultation rounds.

From time to time, King Frederic, who had become
a dear friend, paid him visits, bringing warmth
to his heart. As time went by, things changed in
his kingdom. Some subjects approached
him trustfully with their concerns,
some servants became friendlier,
and with his queen he had new
and remarkable conversations.
More and more he managed
to listen to his little advisors in the
evenings and even when things
weren't quite yet the way he wished
for, he could be at peace with that.

Sometimes it happened that an
experience was too painful.
In those moments when the
pain felt too heavy to bear, he
would yearn for the times when
he knew no such sorrows,
living in peaceful certainty that
everything within him was just
fine, and it was only others who
behaved wrongly or poorly.

For example, when his queen or the growing royal children said something to him that hurt a lot.

If only he had never begun to heed the council of the tiny advisors! Then he traveled back to Frederic right away and recovered for a while in his royal garden. They had long talks to find out why he was so bothered by what he had heard. Archibald was allowed to show how angry he was about what had happened and Frederic gave him the time he needed for that. After a while he could sense that underneath the anger was a great sadness. Oh dear, oh dear, he could not have endured that without Frederic by his side. It was so good to hear from him that every time he went through these terrible feelings, he took a big step forward on his way to becoming a beloved and happy king!

As time went by, he himself could tell that the challenging feelings didn't last as long as they had in the beginning. Before he knew it, while gazing at one of the beautiful roses, that little fellow appeared within him once more. Oh, what wondrous sensations he could evoke!

When, in the evening, a messenger on horseback came from his kingdom to bring a letter from his queen, assuring him of her love and asking him to come back to her soon, he realized what a gift it had been to expose himself to all of these troubles. She had never said or written anything like that to him before!

During their evening stroll before his departure, the two kings reflected on Archibald's first visit to Frederic with a chuckle and they agreed on what a good idea that had been!

 # Epilogue

If you would like to have a circle of these little advisors around you, I invite you to check out our online *Gefühlsmonster Scan*[6] for your own evening reflection. This is an exercise where you can reflect and end your day in a constructive way. You will find detailed instructions there as well.

More royal exercises with the little colorful creatures can be found in my book *Leading with Empathy*[7].

If you want to understand even better how to deal with the little colorful creatures, you can find more in my book *Sometimes Feelings are Monsters*[8]. Or visit our *Gefühlsmonsters Academy* and learn together with other *queens and kings*[9].

---

6 Gefühlsmonster online toolbox: scan.gefuehlsmonster.de
7 Available in bookstores (ISBN 978-3-347-18597-5) and in the Gefühlsmonster Shop: *gefuehlsmonster-shop.de*
8 Available in bookstores (ISBN 978-3-347-37040-1) and in the Gefühlsmonster Shop: *gefuehlsmonster-shop.de*
9 *gefuehlsmonster.de/en – Currently workshops in English available upon request.*

Epilogue

Read more here:

   *gefuehlsmonster.de/en/seminars-workshops/*

And if you want to have the little advisors at home, you can find them here:

   *gefuehlsmonster-shop.de*

I would like for you to tell me about your royal experiences. And if there is no King Frederic at hand, you are very welcome to talk to me! You can reach me by e-mail at:

lhc@gefuehlsmonster.de

# Acknowledgement

It's been a few years since I read the beginning of my fairy tale to my dear colleague Antje Vorndran, and I could see how she shared my enthusiasm – and how she desperately wanted to hear the continuation, even the resolution of this story, which unfortunately was far from being coherent for myself at that time. I had to make her and myself wait, while I worked on the continuation which I had to put aside often.

Antje was the first one who read the finally finished story and encouraged me to publish it now.

My thanks go on to my dear colleagues who acted as proof-readers: Monika Knauer-Walter, Armin Rau, Liana Heinrich, Ragna Kirberg-Siemer, Thomas Fehr, Andre Motzkus.

Dr. Katrin Prüfig, my esteemed media trainer, then encouraged me to actually publish the fairy tale as a small book. She also pointed out that something important was missing in the first version, namely how Archibald felt about the strange narration of Frederic.

His feelings, his "tugging at his hair" and his deep sighs show how he slowly gets used to these new ways of looking at things, which he only endures because he wants an improvement of his own situation. His slowly emerging understanding, that it's not about the "stupid" subjects, but about educating the king. Katrin's contribution removed the last stumbling block of the story.

Acknowledgement

Thank you to my editor, Erik Kinting, who immediately agreed to publish this fairy tale as a small book, and returned my draft edited with his usual quality and speed. The fact that I'm happy with his respectful, minor corrections, and that at one point we are able to agree on my version, is now almost routine in our collaboration.

Many thanks also to the graphic designer Sabine Abels, who contributed brilliant ideas on how to give the fairy tale a worthy appearance – and incorporated all the subsequent changes and improvements with her usual patience.

And last, but not least: thanks to my son Christian, my best proof-reader, who noticed every inconsistency in comprehensibility and every little thing in text and design that needed improvement. To him I owe not only the *Gefühlsmonster*s, but also the magnificent depiction of the two kings that adorns every page of the fairy tale.

For the English version: Thank you to my dear friend, Willow Toccata, who agreed on the spot to completely revise this text again to maintain the "fairy tale" feel of the original German text.

In closing something about myself

What I can feel makes me alive,
lets me participate in what is happening around me
and is a guideline for my path.

My Son, Christian Corona, gave me the *Gefühlsmonster®* Cards as an invaluable gift (video about the history of the *Gefühls-monster*s here: youtube.com/gefuehlsmonster). These cards really unleashed my urge to explore, and after 18 years of using the cards in their current form, I can justifiably say that they are an exceptionally helpful tool for initiating conversations about feelings with ease. They also help to understand oneself better and to get back into a state of action more quickly in difficult situations.

The longer I work with the *Gefühlsmonster®* Cards, the more I appreciate the lightness and humor they bring to conversations, even and especially with difficult feelings. And I appreciate the mutual understanding that is strengthened by the pictures. During my professional career, first as a mediator, then teaching mediation and then as a consultant for individuals and organizations, the *Gefühlsmonster*s have gained great

importance for me. They have inspired me to intensively investigate how I deal with feelings, both in my clients and in myself.

Nowadays we can make our own choices for how to deal with our emotions. We can learn which feelings have to do with ourselves, which have to do with our past experiences and which have to do with the present moment. This gives us the freedom not to let difficult feelings limit us or stop us from doing what we think is right and important.

A conscious and reflective approach to feelings leads to welcoming all feelings. This takes some practice and the will to learn. And it works better with encouraging guidance.

I hope that Archibald's story could bring some of these aspects closer to you!

With best regards

Lilli Höch-Corona
Berlin, August 2023
lillihoechcorona.de/en

Zeitfracht Medien GmbH
Ferdinand-Jühlke-Straße 7
99095 Erfurt, Deutschland
produktsicherheit@kolibri360.de